Flourishing
Across the
Spectrum

Flourishing
Across the
Spectrum

The handbook on raising a child
with autism

Bebe Boyse

Spring Publishing

ISBN 978-0-9927587-5-2

Published by Spring Publishing, an imprint of Careertrain Publishing 2016

www.springpublishing.co.uk   hello@springpublishing.co.uk

Printed and bound in Great Britain

Disclaimer

This book is for information purposes only and is not intended as a substitute for legal or other professional services.

Readers are urged to consult a variety of sources and educate themselves fully. The information expressed herein is the opinion of the author, and is not intended to reflect upon any particular person, institution or company.

The author shall have no responsibility or liability with respect to any loss or damage caused by the information or application of the information contained within this book.

Acknowledgements

Firstly I have to thank my son James from whom I have learnt so much. We have had many years of laughter and tears, and without him I would not have been able to write this book.

I would also like to thank my mum for all her support over the years, not only for all the times she looked after James while I was at work but also for her endless love, common sense advice and great listening ear.

Thanks to my partner Paul who has been unwavering in his love and support through the highs and the lows.

A final thanks to Jules for her long term and much valued friendship – including great copy editing skills – and my other mastermind girlies who said 'Write a book'...which I did, and I hope it is of value to all who read it.

Thank you all x

Contents

Foreword

When I was first asked if I would write a foreword for this book, my mind was immediately cast back to a sunny weekend way back in the late 1990s. Bebe and I had known each other just a few months as colleagues and were working extra hours to complete an important project. Keeping us by turns focused and then pleasantly distracted was the delightful James, a wide eyed bundle of life just about two years old.

Bebe and I did not know each other well enough at the time for her to reveal to me the challenges that I have since discovered she was confronted with every day, loving and nurturing a child with such extraordinary gifts and talents; a child with unique and complex needs, so many of which, it seems, became apparent only with the wisdom of hindsight.

Reading their story all these years later, I am humbled to think of the professionalism that she showed throughout those years that we worked together, never giving away the fact that she was, most days, surviving on snatches of sleep and large doses of starlight as she and her little boy gazed together at the night sky waiting for his senses to finally be soothed to sleep.

Back then, I knew Bebe as a pioneering spirit, someone with rock solid values under-pinning her years of experience working with people with learning difficulties. She commanded considerable respect amongst colleagues for her enlightened views on what mattered most in services for people with special needs and, as I reflect on the woman that I knew then, I see all the budding qualities that enabled her to so successfully rise to the challenge of being a single parent to a child whose development would, over the years, challenge many of the usual expectations of parenthood.

Parents with children on the autism spectrum will understand that nothing quite prepares you for the very unique experience of discovering that your child's understanding of what works best for them is often very different from your own and, indeed, very different from every other parents' views. Behaviours perceived by others as naughty or rude are often in fact valiant attempts by a child living with the challenges of autism, to express themselves in the only way they know how. Understanding this is the first step towards adapting to a different parenting style.

This handbook is an honest, raw account of the adaptions that were required once it became apparent that conventional parenting was not enabling James' spirit to flourish. Whether you are yourself a parent, carer, sibling or teacher of a child living with autism – or indeed if you are none of the above but merely curious, Bebe's books offer valuable insights, sharing as she does her own experience of gradually coming to understand James' unique experience of the world; learning through the successes and mistakes, learning through laughter and tears but, most of all, learning through the journey. It is with tremendous pride that I commend this book to you the reader.

Karen Carpenter.

Karen Carpenter is a Mental Health Professional with over 30 years' experience working with people with mental health difficulties, learning disabilities and autism. She is also a qualified performance and life coach. Karen currently works as a freelance consultant, trainer and interim manager and has her own coaching practice based in Shropshire.

Introduction

Flourishing Across the Spectrum is based on the journey I have experienced as a parent, and includes my reflections on raising a child with autism.

It builds on a series of short books that I wrote for different age groups; I have now amalgamated the series in this handbook as a single reference point or guide, regardless of how old your child is. This handbook still tells the story and the lessons learnt but also covers some of the things you may encounter with guidance on how to handle various situations.

My approach is about valuing difference and highlighting strategies to cope with societal norms. Flourishing Across the Spectrum focuses on the unique experience of having a child with autism, and asks questions such as 'Is this normal behaviour for a child of 6 months, 8 months, 12 months etc.?' and 'Well, what is NORMAL[1] anyway?'

Important: before proceeding, I would like to impress upon you the diversity of challenges in the autism spectrum. The spectrum is huge, and each individual child will experience it in a different way and have a range of difficulties that are unique for them.

My son has hyper sensitivity with touch, taste, smell, hearing and sight. He has some repetitive behaviours and struggles with eye contact and social situations. Also he has increased anxiety in any change to his usual routine. Another child could have additional challenges around spatial awareness, fixated

---

[1] Normal is defined as: 'Conforming to a standard. Usual, typical or expected.' (Oxford English Dictionary)

gaze and verbalising but have no difficulties around change of routine. Another child could have repetitive behaviours, no eye contact and communication difficulties with additional learning difficulties or disabilities or impaired cognitive functioning.

Every child is different.

Please note also that I am not a medical professional. I am writing this purely from the perspective of a parent who has thirty years' experience of working with children, young people and families, and a background in psychology.

Finally, my mother and I often commented that each new stage in my son's development presented new challenges. I will share these here with you, to help mothers and fathers all over the world understand that there are alternative ways of bringing up children that are based on a fundamental understanding of that child's individual needs.

I got it wrong many, many, times. I constantly wonder whether my misunderstanding of my son has damaged him, but he appears very resilient in his own way. I feel blessed to have learnt so much from him.

Bebe Boyse

Section One
What are we talking about?

"Write to be understood.
Speak to be heard.
Read to grow"

Lawrence Clark Powell

What is autism?

You will hear terms such as autistic, Asperger's, spectrum disorders, high functioning autism, atypical autism and so on. These are all one and the same thing, and the now commonly used term is autism spectrum.

Autism spectrum is very different to ADHD (attention deficit hyperactivity disorder) and so not to be confused. Please note that a child might have autism spectrum *and* ADHD, or autism spectrum *and* any other difficulty or disorder.

As mentioned, how one child experiences autism spectrum will be very different from another. However, there are three main areas of difficult in autism spectrum:

1. communication and social interaction

2. behaviour

3. sensory experience.

The definition that I use is:

Someone with differences in neurological processing that can affect their sensory experiences, their communication and social interaction, and their behaviour.

(Bebe Boyse, 2014)

The condition, therefore, is about how the brain processes information which affects how the child experiences the world around them and how they then respond to that.

You may be asking what causes autism spectrum? The research is ongoing but to date scientists have determined that there are a number of genes that can contribute to autism. For some families they will find that autism spectrum runs in the family and for others it might be a one off malformed gene. The ongoing debate is around what causes the malformation of genes, and that is where you will read about vaccinations and other factors causing autism.

This handbook does not dwell on the how and why but focuses on the delights and challenges of parenting, with hints and tips to get through the day to day obstacles that you will face.

On a personal note I really surprised myself in terms of the beliefs, hopes, wishes and expectations I had about being a parent. I had always thought of myself as someone who was very laid back, but I found that I departed from this in having a baby.

Where did these expectations come from? Glossy magazines? Films? Books? TV? Family? All of the above, or just some?

I don't know, but I had them and they have all been challenged over the last 21 years.

Having learnt many lessons, I now very clearly take the view:

Take each day as it comes. Do your best to work with the challenges that are presented on that day. They will all be different. Resolve to enjoy the ride.

I have on many occasions been lulled into a false sense of security that I can anticipate what will happen, and I have been proven wrong so many times.

In my view being a parent of a child with autism requires four key things:

1. *Being open-minded*

2. *Being flexible and responsive*

3. *Being forward-thinking and non-judgemental*

4. *Seeing the beauty in the small things.*

These qualities seem to have served me well over recent years. I just wish I had applied them earlier.

Key points and summary about autism spectrum

- There are many terms that are used interchangeably but autism spectrum is the preferred term.

- Every child is different.

- Every child experiences the autism spectrum in a different way.

- The autism spectrum is about how the brain processes information from the world around us.

- There are three areas of difficulty for the child:
  - communication and social interaction
  - behaviour
  - sensory experiences.

- Take each day at a time, they will all be different!

- Nurture the personal qualities that will help you stay calm and supportive for your child.

Reflections on the autism spectrum

❀ *If someone asked you what the autism spectrum was, how would you describe it in an easy to understand way?*

❀ *What were your expectations, hopes, wishes and dreams of being a parent for the first time?*

❀ *What personal traits do you want to nurture in yourself that will help you and your child over the coming years?*

First indications

Cracks soon started to appear in the wall that I had built around my expectations of having a baby and what family life should be like. I knew instinctively that the wall was holding back a flood of emotions that I wasn't sure I could handle. I kept trying to patch up the cracks and live in a state of denial.

So what were these cracks? What were the first indications?

For my son it was a combination of feeding issues with associated weight loss, lack of sleep, crying, sensory sensitivity with touch and sound, and constipation.

For you and your child it might be other things.

What makes it more unclear is that, on their own, some of these issues are quite common for babies. It is on reflection when you look back at the whole picture you can see the indicators forming a pattern.

Feeding and weight loss

I had chosen to have a home birth and it all went very smoothly. The first few weeks trundled on with the usual midwife and health visitor appointments. I recovered well from the birth. I was enjoying being a new mum.

As the weeks moved on it became apparent that James (my son) was losing weight not gaining it. I was advised by the health visitor that I wasn't producing enough milk and in order to enable James to thrive I would have to move to bottle feeding. He seemed much happier with the bottle and I had to suspend my desire to do all things natural including breastfeeding. That was the first major crack in the ideological bubble in which I was living!

Sleeplessness

I was under the misguided assumption that once James was feeding well his sleeping pattern would improve. I had expected unsettled nights but whole nights without sleep was exhausting. There appeared to be no link between the amount of milk that James had and his ability to rest.

In the first few years James would wake anytime from 11pm and be unsettled for the rest of the night. During these nights he was not awake and calm, he was awake and distressed. In fact, it was four years before he slept through the night without having to get up. Four years, three months and two days. Not that I was counting!

It became increasingly important that I rid myself of the pressure to have a house that was clean and tidy. The priority became sleep. In order to have the patience to settle a distressed child in the middle of the night you need to ensure that you look after yourself, eat well and to get rest whenever you can.

Crying

I was hugely underprepared for the crying. As a single mum the comforting was down to me and nothing I tried appeared to help, with one exception. If it was warm enough and not raining, standing outside under our tree and looking up at the stars was the one thing that calmed the crying. It took me six months to realise this.

I came to love those summer evenings when we could do this. I also cherished the warmer autumn evenings when it was still possible. In fact, being outside and looking at the stars still works today and James often comments on how twilight is the best time of day for him.

Touch sensitivity

Then there was 'nappygate' as I called it. Nappy changing time was a battle of wills. Who would have thought that a baby could be so determined to avoid wearing a nappy? I tried all sorts, from nappy changing in different rooms, different nappies, different people changing the nappies, putting it on by stealth from behind, and no nappy (very messy, to be avoided!). In the end I just had to deal with the bruises from his high speed piston legs. Good grief that boy has powerful legs!

I secretly prayed for the day when nappies were no longer needed.

Hindsight is a wonderful thing and I now know that 'nappygate' was actually about James' touch sensitivity. In later years this sensitivity has translated into other clothing items and objects; it was a blessing when James could say what he didn't like about a certain texture. Often it would be a sensation with an associated noise.

Some children with autism are not able to verbalise so it will be a process of elimination to work through what the actual issue might be. For James it was more about the noise than the feel of certain things when rubbing together. These were sounds that I couldn't hear but for James with his hyper sensitive hearing, it was unbearable to him.

I have found that the skill in parenting a baby with neurological differences, where those differences affect how they experience the world, is to learn to understand what they are communicating to you.

Suspend your understanding and belief about what is a 'normal' experience. Realise that your baby is going through something altogether different.

Identify what the issue is and what you can do to change the experience. For example with 'nappygate' I tried many different things to help with the nappy problem. However, it never occurred to me that it was the material that was the issue. Yes, I tried different nappies but they were all disposable nappies, made of the same or similar material. I never tried a terry cloth nappy. I should have.

Constipation

A lot of research indicates a link between autism and gastrointestinal (GI) problems. I didn't know this at the time and I thought I just had a baby that struggled with constipation. The GI problems can be with diarrhoea, constipation, gastric pain or food sensitivity.

There is some debate among academics about the cause. Is it the behaviour, the stress and the anxiety that causes the GI problems or do the GI problems cause pain which then results in behaviour which tries to communicate this? I firmly believe that it is the latter; in fact, I believe that all behaviour is a means of communicating something.

There is, however, common agreement that more research is needed into why there is a link between GI problems and autism spectrum. To read more about the research have a look at some of the articles on my webpage: www.spectrumparenting.net

Outings

Going out to the park was a pleasure; I have many beautiful photos of James being held and looking up at the trees. This of all things was the one reliable way to calm him down if he was upset, to go outside and look at the trees.

Going out to the shops or to a cafe was a completely different story. It truly amazes me how nonverbal babies can clearly communicate their dislikes. I found I had to do shopping when my baby was asleep and hope that he didn't wake up while we were out. I avoided or declined invitations to go to restaurants as I knew that it would be unpleasant for him, me and all the other diners present.

The cracks were definitely there: weight problems, constant crying, sleepless nights, constipation, touch and sound sensitivity. There were many good times too, many giggles, many quiet moments enjoying watching James and many lovely walks in the park with the dogs.

Summary of first indicators

- When a parent stands back and looks at the WHOLE picture there are usually some common early indicators of autism spectrum.

- These can be (but are not exclusive to): feeding issues, sleeplessness, inconsolable crying, gastro-intestinal problems etc.

- Suspend your understanding and belief of what is normal.

- Try alternatives to establish what the issue might be.

- Be kind to yourself; ensure you get sleep, healthy food and a rest whenever you can.

- See the beauty in the small things.

Reflections on first indicators

❀ What am I doing to look after myself?

❀ What else can I do?

❀ What is the pattern of first indicators for my child?

Being worried and what to do about it

As parents we worry, we all worry; I think it is quite a natural thing. However, when I find myself in this state I like to remind myself of the following quote:

> *'Worrying is like being in a rocking chair,*
> *it gives you something to do*
> *but gets you nowhere!'* (Source unknown)

I find it helpful to focus on the specific thing that is worrying me. Sometimes it is hard to find the source of the concern because I displace my anxiety onto other things. For example, I will think that I am concerned about something coming up at work, or a conversation that I need to have with someone or worrying about payment of a bill.

Consciously I have to come up with a solution to each of the divergent topics that pop into my head. I then ask myself 'Am I still worried?' Usually, after three or four side-track issues, I get to the source.

In finding the source of concern I then have to unpick it. For example, I am worried that James has not made any vocalisation or noise and he is now nine months old. I then ask myself: is this usual? Is this typical? How do I find out? Who can I get advice from? And most importantly what can I do about it?

To this end, as a way of supporting parents who are worried, I have compiled a short list of typical stages of development for children between the ages of 0-2. This is a guide only and is based on my reading and experience. It is not a definitive, but I found it helpful when I have been worried and thought, 'Should I be?'

My worrying process:

1. I have identified the TRUE source of my concern

2. I have used the guide below to identify whether the concern is within normal ranges of development

3. I have found that it is UNUSUAL

4. I have decided where to go for help: a medical professional such as GP or health visitor. In talking to them it is best to give specific information about the concern e.g.: what, why, when, how, how often.

Typical development

These are typical milestones for development your baby should go through. You can use them as a yardstick if you have concerns about your baby's progress.

Typical development: 0 – 12 months

Senses: (Sight, hearing, touch, taste, smell)

Within the first few days and weeks a baby starts to focus their eyes. Feeding close up (either breast or bottle) helps a baby develop their eye muscles and to focus on a 20-30 cm distance. A baby of this age prefers black and white contrast to be able to develop their focusing ability (up to 3 months old).

A baby in their first 12 weeks will typically respond to noises as their hearing develops. Singing, talking, reading while holding your baby close all help. A baby will be picking up on tone and rhythms not the words (up to 3 months old).

3–6 months will see a baby exploring objects by putting things in their mouth.

By 9 months the eyes have developed. A baby will have full colour vision and be able to track moving objects.

By 9 months a baby will turn when they hear voices in a room. Babies at this age also tune into tone of voice and rhythms rather than words.

Communication and social interaction:

Within the first 12 weeks a baby's facial muscles will start to develop and they will begin to smile and respond to the things around them.

3-6 months will see a baby being able to copy sounds and some actions.

In the first 6 months a baby will start to vocalise, i.e. they will start to make new and different noises.

By 9 months a baby will begin to respond to 'no' and their own name.

By 12 months a baby can vocalise double syllable sounds like mama, dada, caca.

Behaviour:

Between 3-6 months you might notice your baby reaching for toys or objects. This shows physical development as well as cognitive development and curiosity.

Physical development:

The first 12 weeks will see a baby develop their neck muscles and they will start to pick their head up.

There is general muscle development in this period where a baby will start to wriggle, kick and roll.

3-6 months a baby will start to grasp and then be able to hold objects.

By around 6 months old a baby is likely to be passing objects from hand to hand.

By 9 months a baby might sit unsupported and become more mobile, for example moving backwards and forwards and shuffling on their bottom.

At 9 months a baby might be able to stand for a short time while holding onto an object e.g. a table or chair.

By 12 months a baby will be able to let go of objects or hand an object to someone else.

A 12 month old may enjoy feeding themselves or holding small pieces of food in their hands and putting it in their mouths.

Typical development: 12 – 24 months

Senses: (Sight, hearing, touch, taste, smell)

Babies from 12-18 months can be very fussy about what they eat and maybe only eat the same favourite foods. This is an indication of the development of their sense of taste and smell.

Communication and Social interaction:

Between the ages of 12–18 months a baby will start to vocalise around 6–20 recognisable words.

By 24 months a child can usually put two words together.

At ages 12-18 months a baby will show specific preference for certain people or toys.

Behaviour:

Between 12–18 months a baby commonly cries when left by their mother, father or carer.

At this age a baby can also be shy or anxious around strangers.

Physical development:

By 18 months a baby is starting to walk and generally becoming more independent. For example at 18 months a baby may want to dress and feed themselves.

Hand to eye coordination has also developed to a stage where a child can place toy bricks on top of each other and place items in holes (like credit cards in dvd players!).

Physical development is rapid in these first few years. By age two a child can usually throw balls, kick, stand on their tiptoes and climb onto things, walk or crawl upstairs (the skills to come down stairs develop later), hold a crayon or brush to do a painting and so on.

Potential indicators of autism

The following are indicators that your baby may be on the autism spectrum.

Indicative development: 0 – 24 months

Senses: (Sight, hearing, touch, taste, smell)

By 6 months your baby is not responding to noises or has an extreme/distressed response to noise.

By 9 months your baby does not show an interest in any toys.

By 12 months your baby shows no interest in tracking moving objects.

By 18 months your baby shows no visible response when there are voices in a room.

By 24 months your baby cries when touched or is distressed when touching new textures.

DO NOT worry about fussy eating, this is normal. This is an indication of the development of their sense of taste and smell.

Communication and social interaction:

By 9 months your baby is not responding to the things around them including people and objects.

By 9 months your baby is not babbling, copying sounds and some actions.

By 12 months your baby does not respond to simple commands like 'no' or their own name.

By 12 months your baby is not vocalising anything.

By 24 months your baby has fewer than 15 words in their vocabulary and does not use 2 word sentences.

DO NOT worry if your child shows specific preference for certain toys, as this is normal up to the age of 5.

Behaviour:

Between 12–24 months your baby does not show any emotion around strangers; it is normal for a child of this age to be shy or anxious.

By 24 months your baby is physically able but not showing any interest in exploring the world around them.

By 24 months your child is able but does not want to hold a spoon or handle food during meal times.

By 24 months your child still gets distressed by new textures like sand or paint or new clothing, or they cry when touched.

By 24 months your baby refuses to cuddle and shows no affection.

By 24 months your baby is still distressed every night and difficult to console.

This is not an exhaustive list and I am not a medical professional. However, this may provide some help in allaying any fears you may have, or in confirming that you might need to seek the opinion of a medical expert. Children with autism may not display all of the above, but certainly if you have concerns in more than three of the different areas, then talk to someone about it.

Your checklist of development (0-24 months)

Use the checklist on the next page to assess your child's development in relation to **typical** sensory development, communication and behaviour.

Area of development	✔	When
Focuses their eyes		
Responds to noises		
Puts things in their mouth		
Tracks moving objects		
Begins to smile		
Copies sounds and actions		
Responds to 'no' and their name		
Vocalises sounds like mama, dada…		
Reaches for toys		
Grasps and holds toys		
Explores the world around them with touch, taste and sight		
Passes things from hand to hand		
Feeds themselves / holds small pieces of food		
Has around 20 recognisable words		
Is able to put words together		
Shows specific preference for toys and people		
Enjoys cuddles and affection		
Cries when left by primary carers		
Is shy or anxious around strangers		

Reflections on typical development

❋ What process do you use to identify what you are REALLY worried about?

❋ What is your biggest concern about your child at the moment?

❋ What are you going to do about it?

Section Two
Bringing up a child with autism

*If things are going right,
don't touch anything,
don't change anything
In fact, maybe, don't even breathe"*

Autism United 2014

Single parenting and co-parenting

Is it me?

For a long time I thought 'maybe this is the same with all babies' but I was quickly disabused of this belief when I would see mothers at play groups or in coffee shops, with happy and content babies. Then I had the thoughts *'it's me' 'it's my parenting style' 'they must just be better mums than me' 'I'm doing something wrong'*.

I established the belief that I was the issue. I persevered with going out to coffee shops and joining a baby group. But I just couldn't sustain it, James was so unhappy, anxious or withdrawn I stopped going. Emotionally I swung between telling myself that I had stopped because James was unhappy to the other hand of telling myself that I was weak-willed with poor discipline.

Authoritarian parenting

People who believe that authoritarian parenting is the most effective method would say that I should, regardless of how long it takes, insist on certain behaviours in public. Also, that I should provide punishment if my child does not adhere to those behaviours. Indeed, some people adamantly believe that the parent should be in control at all times and determine what happens and when.

I have, over the years, been surrounded by people with this 'authoritarian parenting' belief. It is hard when you fundamentally believe in a different approach when being with other parents who are authoritarian. I have a child who struggles with new situations and will demonstrate this through screaming or crying. Some parents or adults stand in judgement about both your child and your parenting approach. They can be silent in their judgement but even without words can make their thoughts known.

An important aspect about parenting together is that each adult will have their own style. Regardless of this they should work hard on being consistent with their children. Together both parents should have a shared philosophy on what is important in bringing up their children.

A further complicating factor is when there is shared but separate parenting. Effective, open, honest communication is essential. The fact that the adults are separated may mean that relationships are already difficult. However, it is essential for the sake of the child to have an agreed consistent approach to parenting.

Where an authoritarian style exists alongside another style in a family then conflict between parents is likely. How this manifests will differ depending on the personalities within the family. However, most commonly when the authoritarian parent is there then that style becomes the dominant driver in the family dynamic. A parent with a permissive style will in some ways seek to avoid the conflict and try to smooth things over at a later stage.

The effect this has on the child varies. For some children they just adapt and behave differently when different parents are there. For other children they play one parent off against the other. Other children might retreat into themselves as a coping mechanism and so on.

I have learnt that children are very adept at picking up on discourse, disagreements or divergences in parenting styles.

Children know how to get a reaction from each adult and very often will have no hesitation in getting a response either positive or negative.

I have also learnt that it is important to know yourself and be aware of what winds you up. Understand what your pressure points are. If you have an awareness of this I find that you can be calmer in dealing with your own emotional reaction when a child presses those buttons!

Discipline

In my experience of raising a child with autism I firmly believe that a child doesn't fully understand social rules and norms. Or if they do understand them they are having such sensory experiences that they are physically, emotionally or cognitively unable to comply.

Punishment for behaviour that is deemed by another to be inappropriate will not be understood by the child and therefore the punishment will have limited, if any effect. My belief is this:

A child's behaviour is a way of communicating a need and our job as parents is to understand what that need is and then respond appropriately.

Parenting techniques

I have taken some traditional parenting strategies and gone on to explain the difference that needs to be applied when you have a child with autism.

1. **Labelled praise:** This is where a parent gives very specific feedback to the child on what they are pleased about in

terms of behaviour. This is always to be encouraged as the more we give positive praise to our children the better. I like to see this as celebrating the small moments.

For example when we had a nappy changing time that was not a battle I would be so happy. I started off demonstrating this by doing raspberry bubbles on James' belly; this resulted in screams and minor meltdowns. I then celebrated by big cuddles, which resulted in face scratching. I then toned down the celebration, but a celebration none the less to just big smiles and a calm voice and singing nursery rhymes.

The lesson here is that you need to find out what your baby responds to in terms of affection and praise as every child will be different.

2. **Ignoring minor misbehaviour:** Again this is to be encouraged, however for a child with autism the parenting strategy is slightly different in that I think we need to relax our views and expectations on what behaviour is 'acceptable' and 'not acceptable'.

   For example we may want our child to share toys with other children or siblings, but for a child with autism this may be incredibly difficult. If a child has lined up all the toys in a specific order for them and a sibling, friend or indeed an adult comes along and alters the order this may result in frustration, anger or a meltdown for a child with autism. It would be futile to give punishment to your child for this behaviour.

The key is to understand and accept the need that the child has. Ultimately, we should see behaviour as a way of communicating a need.

3. **Time outs:** For some children where this is applied immediately, consistently and calmly then this can be an effective strategy. However for children with autism time outs are invariably ineffective.

   The reason for this is that the child is not demonstrating the behaviour to be defiant or intentionally difficult. They are demonstrating the behaviour as a way of meeting an internal requirement for order, structure, routine, sensory stimulation or simply to understand their environment. Providing a timeout will not be understood nor will the alternative behaviour that the parent is suggesting.

   Also a child with autism quite often likes to spend time alone and therefore this strategy may have the unintended consequence of reinforcing the behaviour. The child may understand that a time out will come and this is what is wanted by the child and therefore they may demonstrate the unwanted behaviour more often.

4. **Focus on prevention of misbehaviour:** Parenting guides often give examples of knowing when your child might become tired or hungry and pre-empting this. Again this is to be encouraged. However when parenting a child with autism the key is to understand the unique nature of your child's needs.

- Do they need time alone in a calm state?

- Do they need sensory stimulation to manage their hyper sensitivity?

- Do they need a significant amount of time to prepare for new situations?

- Do they need time to think about something before they can talk about it?

- Do they need to try different textures and experiences several times before they feel comfortable with them?

So the list can go on. Importantly when you have a child with autism the strategy is to know what your child needs to feel safe, calm and comfortable. Then do that.

5. **Take time and do nothing:** Take time to just be with your child, not talking or guiding or doing anything, just being with them. I used to spend hours laying on the floor next to James watching him play with his toy cars or his push along train set. Sometimes he would ask me to join him in lining up his cars in order.

Those are lovely moments when your child reaches out to you. Also, it is useful to just observe what your child enjoys doing. It may help with your understanding.

6. **Look after yourself:** There is much research which indicates that parental stress has a significant impact on parenting ability.

Acknowledge how you are feeling and do all you can to have some time to yourself to de-stress.

- If you are tired, take time to sleep, whenever you can.

- If you are angry, take time out to get to a calmer state.

- If you are skipping meals, don't. You need all the energy you can muster.

- Try to do something each day that makes you laugh. This could be anything from a phone call to a favourite programme or, as was the case for me, watching James himself with his little mannerisms.

- Appreciate the small things. The unexpected and rarely given radiant smile does it every time for me.

Summary of single parenting and co-parenting

- Each adult will have their own parenting style. Know yours.

- It is most important to be consistent with your child.

- Have a shared philosophy on what is important in bringing up your child.

- Know your pressure points and have strategies to calm yourself.

- Remember your child will be experiencing the world in a very different way and may be physically, emotionally or cognitively unable to comply with societal norms. This requires empathy not punishment.

- Behaviour is a way of communicating a need. Our job as parents is to understand what that need is and respond appropriately.

- Understand and accept why your child does certain things.

- Be aware of the unintended consequences of some parenting strategies.

- Know what your child needs to feel safe calm and comfortable.

- Have quiet time to just observe, and you will learn a lot.

- Be kind and look after yourself.

Reflections on parenting

🌾 What is my dominant parenting style?

🌾 What is most important in raising my/our child?

🌾 What are my pressure points, i.e. what winds me up?

🌾 What strategies do I have to remain calm?

🌾 What are the situations when my child is most calm and comfortable?

🌾 What are the situations that make my child anxious or uncomfortable?

🌾 What routines or behaviour does my child have that makes them happy?

Social rules

Children with or without autism are often keen to please. Some children with autism try to understand the social rules and will ask for or seek explanations about what to do.

The child will, when they understand a certain rule, apply it within the context it has been explained. For example, if a child is taught that you use a knife and fork when eating a school dinner, they will use a knife and fork at school but not in a restaurant or at home.

Things can be taken very literally by a child with autism. For example, if I say 'Please take your ironed clothes upstairs', the child might take and place the clothes at the top of the stairs! If your child wants your attention and you say 'I'll be with you in a minute, I'm just in the bathroom', if you appear three minutes later your child might be quite angry with you.

Invariably they will say things as they see them, without any understanding of what might be socially acceptable to say. For example you may have been talking to your child about the importance of exercise to stay healthy and to eat well in order to not be overweight. If described in concrete terms then this can be understood by a child with autism. What may then happen is that when they see someone who is overweight, they may have no hesitation in saying directly, 'you should do more exercise and eat better because you are fat'.

Your son or daughter will probably think they have been helpful and will not understand your reaction or the reaction of the person on the receiving end.

Use of language

I have found that my use of language is so important. I continually made mistakes in my explanations of situations or how I asked James to do things. I would invariably ask James if he would complete a task for me by saying 'Would you like to...' and his response without fail was 'No'. Over time it became apparent that if I spoke in very specific concrete terms I would get a better response than with a question. For example:

Question: *'Would you like to come on a walk with the dogs?'*

Answer: *'No'*

Alternatively, if I say:

Statement: *'Please put your shoes on as we are going for a walk with the dogs in ten minutes.'*

Answer: *'Ok'*

Similarly, if I say:

Question: *'Will you lay the table for dinner please?'*

Answer: *'No'*

Whereas if I say:

Statement: *'I want you to lay the table for dinner. We will be eating in half an hour.'*

Answer: *'Ok'*

As a general rule a statement of intention is far more effective than a question. For a child with autism in their mind they are giving a direct answer to a direct question. For them it is merely a statement fact.

Summary on social rules and language

- Children with autism can be very concrete in their thinking.

- This way of thinking and processing information can make it difficult for them to understand the nuances of social norms.

- Because information can be processed in such a specific way then the language that you use needs to reflect this.

- Be very clear specific and precise with instructions.

- Use statements of intention rather than ask a question.

Reflection on social rules and language

🌱 What are the difficulties I have encountered with my use of language?

🌱 What social situations does my child struggle with?

🌱 What can I do differently to help my child understand?

What is being communicated through behaviour?

'There is something in everything.'

By this I mean:

1. **If a child screams and reacts violently when touched, then there is a reason for this.**

    They might have super sensitivity to touch or they may experience pain in a different way.

    A baby might demonstrate this, as James did, by:

    - pulling away from cuddles

    - clawing at your face

    - screaming through any bath time

    - resisting being dressed, including having nappies put on

    - screaming at the beach

    - refusing to play with paint or in a sand pit (any messy play is a no go)

    - screaming at meal times

    - refusing to put their hands on the floor etc.

    Here are some things that worked for James and me. With the cuddles, if I let James initiate the first touch he seemed more comfortable to have sustained physical contact.

When James had to be held and was clearly unhappy about it then his favourite blanket was wrapped round him. Plus I always kept his finger nails short! My mum did get a broken nose once when James was wrapped in his blanket but he threw his head backwards and collided with her nose... ouch! Watch out for that one. We quickly learnt which clothes were the preferred items. We tried all sorts of play including painting and playing in the sand pit. But if these were distressing to James we just didn't do them again.

It is important to be open-minded and flexible about what you do and when you do it, and be responsive if things are not going well.

2. **If a child will not touch or play with certain toys then there is a reason for this.**

   It is likely to be a sensory sensitivity such as sound or touch. A toy that we think makes a fun noise could be heard very differently by a child with autism. The volume may be different as well as the pitch. I certainly found that he always preferred the toys that made no noise such as toy cars and tractors.

3. **If a child is unable to sleep through the night, then there is a reason for this.**

   James would cry for hours and the only calming situation was being outside at night looking up at the starry sky. I can understand James' fear or rejection of certain things due to touch or hearing, but to this day I do not understand what woke him from a sleep and kept him awake for hours. Was it a wet nappy? Sometimes yes, sometimes no. Was it an unusual sound? I don't know. Was it nightmares? I don't know. Was it bed clothes feeling uncomfortable? Was it a combination of all of the above on different nights? I don't know, I just know it happened and there would have been a trigger for him.

4. **If your child is constipated or has diarrhoea, then there is a reason for this.**

    Is it the balance in their diet? Is it a food sensitivity? Is it some intestinal infection or related problem or is it linked to autism and anxiety?

5. **Behaviour is a means of communicating something.**

    Your child is behaving in a certain way: screaming; crying; punching; spitting; scratching; smearing, whatever it is. There is a reason for this. A key lesson for me was that often the behaviour was delayed. A child might not display any emotion at the time, but will react at another completely unexpected point. This can make it very difficult to understand what the trigger to the behaviour is.

    Here are the questions I found helpful to ask myself when struggling to find the trigger:

    - What was the behaviour?

    - When did that behaviour start?

    - What was happening at the time?

- Had anything happened in the recent past?
- What is the behaviour telling me?
- Is there a pattern to this?
- What was my response?
- What did I say? Was it clear, calm and concrete?
- What worked in calming the situation?
- What was I expecting and how did the situation differ from my expectations?
- What was it that frustrated me the most?

6. **Keeping a daily journal.**

With hindsight I found keeping a daily journal helped. Sometimes it was soul destroying as there was so much negativity. With a bit of distance and looking back it helped clarify the progress that we made and helped highlight the patterns that were there.

Whatever tool you want to use to gain some objectivity, use it. Objectivity will be your friend. Dealing with behaviour that on the surface is not understandable, can become all consuming.

Summary on communication through behaviour

- Every behaviour is communicating something.

- Take time to try to understand what the issue is.

- Take time and use tools to be objective about situations.

- I recommend writing a journal answering the questions:

– What was the behaviour?

– When did that behaviour start?

– What was happening at the time?

– Had anything happened in the recent past?

- What is the behaviour telling me?

- Is there a pattern to this?

- What was my response?

- What did I say? Was it clear, calm and concrete?

- What worked in calming the situation?

- What was I expecting and how did the situation differ from my expectations?

- What was it that frustrated me the most?

Reflections on communicating through behaviour

❄ Over the past week what behaviour has been displayed?

❄ What response did I have to each behaviour?

❄ What could I have done differently?

Tips on preventing escalation

The 'terrible twos and threes' is a term often used in the UK for the completely normal behaviour of children between the ages of two and three, or eighteen months and four really, where they are becoming more independent and asserting their needs and wishes. The dilemma for children of this age is that their vocabulary hasn't developed sufficiently to be able to say or articulate what they want. Therefore they scream, or cry or throw themselves around.

Children with autism go through exactly the same developmental stages as other children.

The difference is that when a child with autism screams, cries or throws themselves or things around it could be about a distressing environmental situation for them and not just about trying to get a need or wish satisfied.

If your child has a development disability, which is different to autism, then WHEN they go through the stage might be different, but they will go through it.

Once any child gets to a point of extreme behaviour such as throwing things it is too late to intervene effectively. This has been a hard lesson for me. I have had the monkey on my shoulder saying 'You are the adult, do not let a child scream and talk to you in that way'. This has been a pressure point for me and I have had many situations where I have been screaming back. Not such a good role model!

The key to success is identifying when things are starting to escalate and to stop it at that point.

There are many times that I have observed the following in a supermarket, and this is in reference to any child, not a child with autism.

The child is being pushed around in the supermarket trolley. Their senses are immediately stimulated with the wonderful smell of the bakery, usually as soon as you walk in. There are all the bright colours, the buzz of other people shopping.

The parent is trying to decide what to buy or they have seen someone and stopped for a chat or they are on their phone. The child is left to marvel at all the sights, sounds and smells and bright sparkly objects and food covered in sugar that is coloured bright pink or green! The child might start to think: 'I want some of that'. The following invariably happens:

- The parent is distracted and ignores the first pointed finger at an object.

- The parent is distracted and misses the ughhh while pointing at the object.

- The parent is still distracted and ignores the higher pitched ughhh while pointing at the object.

- The parent then moves the trolley on and the child starts banging their feet against the trolley, possibly starts to cry as they are moved further and further away from their object of desire.

- Parent starts to get annoyed and tells them to be quiet and starts to walk more quickly to another aisle.

- Then the screaming or crying becomes full pitched.

- It is too late.

The opportunity to manage the behaviour and understand the demand is gone.

The child wants to try new things and explore their world more, yet they do not have the verbal communication skills or cognitive ability to communicate this. Screaming and crying becomes their primary way of communicating that they want or need something when pointing and vocalising has failed.

Being a parent of any child requires focus and attention, particularly at this point in a child's development which is about trying to understand what a child is communicating.

This is almost the same for a child with autism. The difference is that the child might be **overwhelmed, confused or in pain** by their world and yet they do not have the verbal communication skills or cognitive ability to communicate this. Therefore screaming, crying, rocking, scratching and so on becomes their only method of communicating.

At this point I will introduce my concept of 'autism headgear'. Autism headgear is imaginary glasses and headphones that distort and amplify EVERYTHING. By consciously imagining this, I have more chance of understanding the confusing, overwhelming and frightening place in which we live.

For example, if we were going somewhere new I would do all I could to visit the place first. I would take a few minutes to just LISTEN to everything and then I would imagine these noises being played through a loud speaker. I would then LOOK at everything. I would observe where the light and shade areas are and then I would image things being so much bigger and jumping out. I would then make a decision about how to explain this to James before we went and what we would do if it was too much for James.

Empathy is always going to be your strongest ally. From a place of understanding we can attempt to reduce the factors in the environment that are overwhelming for our children.

Environmental factors

I have been a strong advocate for inclusion during my whole professional and personal life and fundamentally believe that all individuals, regardless of the challenges they face, can live and function in society as long as they get the individual support that they might need.

This does not mean that everyone has to experience everything.

Choice, however that is communicated, needs to be a factor. For example, I don't like the sensation of being on roller skates or ice skates of any description and so I do not go to an ice rink if invited. This is my choice and I make it based on something I know I don't like. Some friends have said to me, 'Oh don't be silly, you'll get used to it, I'll help you round'. I believed this once, but still had an horrendous time. I am now insistent on my choice to decline whenever it is suggested.

This is me as an adult.

What you need to think about as a parent of a child with autism is that there are some environments that are just too much for them. I would suggest for some children supermarkets are just such a place, as are concerts, gigs or sporting events in an arena. Basically any confined space with lots of people, an overload of visual stimulation and a multitude of noises and smells.

You may be thinking it will be great for my child to experience this.

Think again.

Some children with autism will be positively stimulated by these environments and are happy. They might show this by clapping, loudly laughing and rocking. Parenting is about making your child happy and so you would want to experience this with them. However, it is where the behaviour is one of distress that you would avoid the environment.

Put on your autism headgear and consider the environment from your child's perspective and give them a choice. Please note that I am not saying that children with autism should not go out in public places, I am merely advising that you look at each environment from your individual child's perspective and consider whether it will be a positive experience or not.

Safety first

If a situation has escalated and I haven't been able to intervene early enough, then it is important to give James time and most importantly space to let him rant and let off steam. I have had to create a safe space for James to be angry as over the years I have invested a lot in Polyfilla and new items of furniture.

In James's room I changed all the movable objects to soft items and the lampshades from metal and glass to material.

Acknowledge that there will be times when the behaviour has gone past the point of effective intervention and do all you can to ensure that your child is safe.

Listening: not as easy as you might think!

I have also learnt that truly listening and not reacting to the words being used has enabled the de-escalation process to be more successful. I say truly listening because I think we can all be guilty of demonstrating that we might be listening by not talking and being physically present. However, most children have an uncanny knack of knowing whether you are really listening.

To truly listen you need to focus on what is being said and then repeat back what you think you heard. The challenge I have had in the past is that James can take a long time to say what is troubling him. When he is frustrated other things are problematic as well. For example, he does not like me near him, or sitting in his room or on any of his things. I have been told that how I am standing is an issue to him and what I am wearing. So when I am listening for extended periods of time the issue I have is being physically uncomfortable standing in the same position!

Who would have thought that that would be the biggest barrier to listening? It really can be anything; if your mind has wandered to what shall I cook for tea, or I need to call someone, or my feet are killing me, then you are not listening!

What are the triggers?

The bigger key to success is to try and establish what triggers the anger and frustration in the first place. It may seem like nothing to you but to a child it can be very important. Some of the triggers for James have been:

- A toy being out of place.

- Not having a specific pair of socks to wear.

- Not going to school on a teacher training day or bank holiday.

- Any disruption, in fact, to the normal routine: birthdays, summer holidays, Easter etc.

- Free dress day at school or even worse 'themed dress' day at school.

- Not having the same food for breakfast, lunch and dinner.

- Flying insects.

- Trousers not lying right on his shoes.

- The sensation of certain items of clothing on his arms and legs.

- Tying shoe laces.

- Tissue paper.

Your child will have different triggers; you just need to work out what they are. I also found that as James got older his triggers changed. He does like to keep me on my toes!

Summary of preventing escalation

- Know the triggers for your child. They are different for everyone.

- Know what your child does to indicate their emotions are escalating.

- Be alert in all new situations to pick up on clues of raised anxiety.

- Be patient.

- Practice wearing your autism headgear.

- Empathy is your strongest ally.

- Preparation is often the key to success.

- Allow enough time to ensure your child is comfortable before doing anything new.

- Take time to listen to your child.

- Know when a situation has gone too far and look to make your child safe.

Reflection on preventing escalation

🌼 One key thing I need to do differently to prevent escalation is:

🌼 The triggers for my child are:

🌼 What did I learn last time I listened to my child?

Section Three
Working with professionals

"No one can whistle a symphony.
It takes a whole orchestra to play it."

H. E. Luccock

67

First contact with professionals

Your child may have a formal diagnosis of autism spectrum or they may not. Regardless, you will come into contact with a range of professionals throughout the years, from doctors to school teachers. These situations will require you to explain the unique nature of your child's needs. Always remember that you are the expert on your child.

If you find that you and your child are being referred for a more detailed assessment there are a few things you need to be alert to.

1. You are the parent and you know your child best of all. Stay in control. If you think that something sounds wrong or uncomfortable, trust your instinct and challenge it.

2. If you want the help of the medical profession, they will be able to do their job more effectively with the most specific information that you can give them. They will never know your child as well as you do.

3. Small and seemingly inconsequential information can be very important to professionals. Be as detailed as possible about patterns of behaviour.

4. They will use jargon and they won't be aware, in most cases, that they are doing it. Be confident, ask them what they mean and ask for explanations of any unfamiliar terms used (there will be a lot!).

5. Don't be overwhelmed by the assessment process. This is about your child and getting the best possible solutions. Quite often with children with autism who have no other associated disability then the best possible solution is understanding, empathy, consistency and tweaks to the environment.

6. If you are going for further assessment remember a child with autism typically does not respond well to change of routine, new people, new places and very 'odd' questions! Talk to the team doing the assessment about the most sensitive way it can be done. But please be aware that there will, at some point, be a reaction from your child, be ready and prepared.

The system

Entering a system when a person experiences the world in a different way is very challenging for the child but also for the system. James' first experience of a system was 'education'.

At age four James started in reception class. To prepare for the start of school I arranged for James to join the local playgroup. This was to enable him to be more familiar with the routine of getting there, being around other children, understanding what is expected in a classroom type environment and so on.

James managed surprisingly well with playgroup. His coping strategy was to withdraw into himself and be very quiet, to observe from a distance, to do what was asked. At playgroup the language and instruction is directed at each individual child and is usually very clear and specific. This helped James and he was known as just being very quiet.

James would walk to playgroup very willingly as he understood that this was part of his routine. Then James started reception class in the September.

Reception class is intended to be a gentle introductory year to start off primary education in the UK. The difference from playgroup is startling. From a playgroup of 20 children with four members of staff to one classroom with 35 children and one teacher makes all the difference.

James continued with his approach of being very quiet, listening and observing from a distance. However, because there was one teacher with 35 children, the instructions that the teacher gave were not directed at James and they were not always clear and specific.

After a few weeks I had a call from the teacher asking whether I had noticed any hearing problems with James. I hadn't of course as James doesn't have any hearing problems. The irony is that his hearing goes beyond normal ranges!

What his teacher was picking up on was that James wasn't doing what was being asked and he also wasn't looking at her. The lesson here is: as an adult, to describe what you find challenging and don't jump to assumptions about what the issue might be. Because the teacher had raised the hearing issue, a test was duly taken and James was at the top of the ranges measured! Nothing else was ever said.

If the teacher had said 'I have noticed that there is very little eye contact and your son doesn't always follow instructions' this could have led down a very different path toward a formal diagnosis. At any point during this time I could have said 'I am a little worried too, but I don't think it's a hearing issue'. However, I consciously and personally decided not to pursue any diagnosis at this time.

The other pressure that some parents experience is that schools like children to have a diagnosis because in the UK this then attaches a 'Statement of Special Educational Needs' (or SEN) (June 2014). Please note that imminent changes in legislation will mean that the name will change.

Your child will be delightfully known as a S.E.N. child – it should be a child who has additional educational needs, not a S.E.N. child, a small but important difference. This then enables the school to draw down additional funds from the government. These funds are supposed to be used to employ additional support staff for that child in their classroom. However, in some schools the practice is to draw down the funds and disperse the extra support across a range of classes. This is not stated as a criticism of schools but more a comment on how inadequate our education system is at supporting the needs of individual students.

In my years of experience in working with children and family services in the UK, I am acutely aware that the education establishment assumes the power and control. In doing this, children who are non-compliant are often removed, labelled and/or often medicated. My personal challenge was to support James through the education system as safely as possible so that he was not labelled, was not removed and was not medicated.

Being a single mum I had to work to support us and my rock of a mother supported James during the day by taking him to school, picking him up, making dinner and giving him 'unwind' time after school.

If my circumstances were different I would have considered home education. There are many reasons for this but that is for another time. My situation was as it was. Mainstream education was the only option and therefore supporting James to survive it was my priority.

Summary of first contact with professionals and the system

- You are the expert on your child.

- Share information and be as detailed as possible, don't forget the seemingly inconsequential.

- Jargon will be used, ask questions, make sure you understand everything as you will have to explain this later.

- When a child with autism starts school this is challenging for the child and for the school.

- Taking lots of time to prepare your child for their first day is as important as the first day itself.

- Small things will make a big difference for example where the child sits, how instructions are given and limiting external stimuli as much as possible.

- Take time to talk to the teacher about the needs of your child.

To diagnose or not?

I never wanted James to have a label and I have to this day never used a label with him. You may be asking: 'If James never had a diagnosis then how do you know that he has autism?' That happened during a brief relationship which lasted two and a half years.

It was during this time that I was persuaded by my partner to 'get help' managing the behaviour of my son. Following contact with the doctors, James had an appointment with the child and adolescent mental health team. He was assessed and in the pre assessment I explained what I believed to be the case which was that James displayed behaviours on the autism spectrum but that I thought he was at the mild end.

What my new partner said he wanted was advice on the best way for us to manage the behaviours as a partnership. The outcome was confirmation that James was on the autism spectrum but that he was mid-point.

They duly provided advice about what my partner and I should do, which my partner didn't like because it was reiterating what I was already doing and what he actually wanted was permission to control James, which I would never give him.

He also didn't like the fact that they said it was 'Testament to the way I had brought James up that he was in mainstream school at all and that I should carry on doing what I was doing as it was clearly working'.

I was asked whether I wanted a referral to the consultant for a formal diagnosis. I refused.

I believe a diagnosis brings a label, a label brings assumptions. A label brings stigma and a label can get in the way of actually working with the individual things that are challenging for that particular child.

To this day when we talk about his anger, we talk about what makes him angry, what I can do to help; we do not talk about the label of anger management issues linked to autism.

When we talk about his anxiety we talk about what worries him and some solutions; we do not talk about a label.

When we talk about eating, we talk about what stresses him and what I can do to make it better; we do not talk about a label.

When we talk about going somewhere, we talk about it in minute detail to help James feel more comfortable; we do not talk about a label.

There are some things that we do not talk about.

We do not talk about James not wanting to be touched, as the need to cuddle is my need not his.

We do not talk about why he won't say things like 'I love you' as this is my need to hear this and not his.

We also do not talk about the annual build-up of anxiety before a birthday or Christmas, as I put a lot of weight on the importance of birthday and Christmas and James just doesn't like the distinct focus on him or the massive change of routine. I could take the route I have taken with other things like, we now don't go on holiday each year as James just doesn't like 'holidays'. When we have holidayed in the past it has been a source of much stress, trauma, and anxiety. To continue to do this each year, just so that we have had a 'holiday,' became untenable. It became increasingly apparent that this was cruel. The last holiday we had was in 2004.

The biggest question I always ask myself is 'why?' Why do I want James to do that? Why is this important? Why, why, why?

Some Big WHYs:

- Why am I so frustrated and angry?

- Why is a holiday so important?

- Why should we celebrate Christmas and birthdays?

- Why do I not want to go to that appointment?

- Why do both James and I have to go to the shops?

- Why do both James and I have to go to the meal?

The answers to these and all the other whys I have asked help me decide whether the stress and trauma is worth it.

My biggest lesson in parenting is to allow James to enjoy his life. I have to allow James to do the things that make him happy, not me.

A label

Getting a diagnosis and associated label is a personal choice. I am of the opinion that a label of autism spectrum is particularly unhelpful because the spectrum is so big and each child experiences it differently.

Professionals and other adults like hooks to be able to hang things on, such as: 'he does that because he is ASD'. There are two fundamental problems with this statement. The first is that it ultimately dismisses the behaviour without any attempt to understand what the behaviour is communicating. The second issue is 'he is ASD'. No, children are not ASD, they experience autism. They are always a child first.

My view is 'NO, he does that because he is a child that is trying to communicate that something is difficult for him'. A label allows professionals and others to dismiss behaviour and explain it away rather than actually try to understand what the behaviour is telling us.

Early years standards: what you need to know

All children in the United Kingdom attend learning from the age of five through to their teenage years, and are assessed at key stages in relation to their learning and attainment. What is less well known is that children at five years of age are assessed against expected standards of learning, attainment and behaviour. I include below a guide to standards expected, and what I would advise parents to do when the assessment is due with regard to their child with autism.

Even if you are reading this and not resident in the United Kingdom this information may be helpful, as the standards expected are based on research on typical expectations for a five year old.

There are 17 areas included in the 'profile', which is known as the Early Years Foundation Stage (EYFS) profile. As you can see from the guide below, a number of these areas will be particularly challenging for children on the autism spectrum. As a refresher the definition of autism that I am using is:

Someone with differences in neurological processing that can affect their sensory experiences, their communication & social interaction and their behaviour. (Bebe Boyse, 2014)

With this definition in mind I hope that you can appreciate the challenges inherent in this national framework of expectations.

The following is directly referenced from 2016 Early Years Foundation Stage Profile Handbook[2].

Communication and language development:

- Listening and attention: This includes the child's ability to listen in a range of situations, e.g. listening to stories, accurately anticipating key events and responding to what they have heard with relevant comments, questions and actions. They give their attention to what other say and respond appropriately while engaged in another activity.

- Understanding: Children follow instruction involving several ideas or actions. They are able to answer how and why questions about their experiences and in response to stories or events.

- Speaking: Children express themselves effectively, showing awareness of listeners' needs. They use past, present and future forms accurately when talking about events that have happened or are to happen in the future. They develop their own narratives and explanations by connecting ideas or events.

Physical development:

- Moving and handling: Children show good control and coordination in large and small movements. They move confidently in a range of ways, safely negotiating space. They

---

[2] Early Years Foundation Stage Profile 2016 Handbook, Standards and testing agency. ISBN978-1-78315-957-4

handle equipment and tools effectively, including pencils for writing.

- Health and self-care: Children know the importance for good health of physical exercise and a healthy diet and talk about ways to keep healthy and safe. They manage their own basic hygiene and personal needs successfully including dressing and going to the toilet.

Personal, social and emotional development:

- Self-confidence and self-awareness: Children are confident to try new activities, and to say why they like some activities more than others. They are confident enough to speak in a familiar group, will talk about their ideas and will choose the resources they need for their chosen activities. They say when they do or do not need help.

- Managing feelings and behaviour: Children talk about how they and others show feelings, talk about their own and others behaviour and its consequences and know that some behaviour is unacceptable. They work as part of a group or class and understand and follow rules. They adjust their behaviour to different situations and take changes of routine in their stride.

- Making relationships: Children play cooperatively, taking turns with others. They take account of one another's ideas about how to organise their activity. They show sensitivity to others needs and feelings and form positive relationships with adults and other children.

Literacy development:

• Reading: Children read and understand simple sentences. They use phonic knowledge to decode regular words and read them aloud accurately. They demonstrate an understanding when talking with others about what they have read.

• Writing: Children use their phonic knowledge to write words in ways which match their spoken sounds. They also write some irregular common words. They write simple sentences which can be read by themselves and others. Some words are spelt correctly and others are phonetically plausible.

Mathematic development:

• Numbers: Children count reliably with numbers from one to 20, place them in order and say which number is one more or less than a given number. They solve problems like doubling, halving and sharing.

• Shape, space and measures: Children use everyday language to talk about size, weight, position, distance, time and money to compare quantities and objects and to solve problems. They recognise, create and describe patterns.

Understanding of the world:

• People and communities: Children talk about past and present events in their own lives and the lives of family members. They know that other children do not always enjoy the same things and are sensitive to this. They know about similarities and differences between themselves and others and among families, communities and traditions.

- The world: Children know about similarities and differences in relation to places, objects, materials and living things. They talk about the features in their own environments and how environments might vary from one another. They make observations of animals and plants and explain why some things occur and talk about changes.

- Technology: Children recognise that a range of technology is used in places such as homes and schools. They select and use technology for particular purposes.

Expressive arts and design:

- Exploring and using media and materials: Children sing songs, make music and dance and experiment with ways of changing them. They safely use and explore a variety of materials, tools and techniques, experimenting with colour, design, texture, form and function.

- Being imaginative: Children use what they have learnt about media and materials in original ways, thinking about uses and purposes. They represent their own ideas, thoughts and feelings through design and technology, art, music, dance, role play and stories.

How do these apply to children with autism?

Don't make any distinction. Assessors work with every child over a year to determine whether they meet, exceed or do not yet meet each standard. There are four areas of gathering information:

- From parents

- From the child

- From other relevant adults

- From observations

Parents are critical in this process; therefore I have identified particular areas that you may want to consider for discussion with your child's first teacher.

If a child does not yet meet a particular standard, this is called an 'emerging' ability. This is a great term to use with teachers and other professionals.

Listening and attention: This is interesting because very often a child with autism will be listening but the person or people around them may not be aware of this. Usually we identify that someone is listening when they look at us and give non-verbal cues such as a nod of the head or a laugh etc. For a lot of children with autism they find eye contact very difficult and therefore it might be perceived that they are not listening. In fact the reverse is true, in that in order to listen the child has to block out other stimuli such as what they can see and therefore have to look away in order to be able to hear.

This standard expects that a child can *'accurately anticipate key events and respond to what they have heard with relevant comments, questions and actions'*. Very often stories are abstract and out of context and this may present difficulties for some children with autism. They will respond and perhaps ask a question, but in my experience this will be very different to what the assessor may consider 'relevant'. For example, James once said to me that he didn't like Little Red Riding Hood. I asked why, and he said because wolves can't dress up. This is all he would say and he dismissed the story. I consider this very relevant and astute for a four year old but an assessor might need some help to see that this is relevant.

Understanding: *'Children follow instruction involving several ideas or actions.'* If this standard merely said that children can follow instruction – great. However, it states that they are looking for five year olds to be able to follow instructions with many parts to it. In my experience a lot of children, and particularly children with autism, are great when an instruction is clear, precise, non-ambiguous and in small steps. You may have to advise the assessor that they will need to think about the language they use and how they explain what they want.

Speaking: *'Children express themselves effectively, showing awareness of listener's needs'.* If your child is non-verbal the assessor should be able to assess how they express themselves using their own communication method. What concerns me is the emphasis on *'effective'*, however that is judged, and showing awareness of the listeners' needs. For a child with neurological differences just the art of expressing themselves will be a challenge, let alone combining this with showing that they are aware of the listeners' needs!

Moving and Handling: *'Children show good control and coordination in large and small movements. They move confidently in a range of ways, safely negotiating space. They handle equipment and tools effectively, including pencils for writing.'* The ability to demonstrate this will depend wholly on the characteristics of autism that your child has. If they struggle with proprioception (the ability to sense stimuli within the body in relation to position, motion and equilibrium) then this will be difficult. But equally if they have a touch sensitivity this will also be problematic.

Health and self-care: *'Children know the importance for good health of physical exercise and a healthy diet and talk about ways to keep healthy and safe. They manage their own basic hygiene and personal needs successfully including dressing and going to the toilet.'* A child with autism may be able to express the importance of good health. But typically children with autism have difficulties with clothes or dressing and are often not independent in going to the toilet by age five.

Self-confidence and self-awareness: *'Children are confident to try new activities, and to say why they like some activities more than others.'* A lot of children with autism will be reluctant to try new activities and will need to be introduced to them gradually.

Managing feelings and behaviour: *'Children talk about how they and others show feelings, talk about their own and others behaviour and its consequences and know that some behaviour is unacceptable.'* This standard presents a fundamental difficulty for children with autism. Partly because the prompts and cues that we provide to children through our language is so far removed from what a child is experiencing they are unable to say what they are feeling. Then the standard goes on to say that the child can: *'work as part of a group or class and understand and follow rules'*. A difficulty in understanding social rules is a classic characteristic of a child with autism. *'They adjust their behaviour to different situations and take changes of routine in their stride.'*

The standards continue with making relationships, reading and writing, numbers and measures, shape and space, people and communities, the world, technology, exploring and using media and materials, and being imaginative.

Why is there such a need for all children to comply with this? Can we not allow our children to be different and be able to learn from each other? Surely there is value in all children being encouraged to learn important qualities such as tolerance, acceptance and difference.

I would advise that you work hard with your preferred education setting to ensure that they have an inclusivity policy. This means that the people working in that setting have learnt the qualities of tolerance, adaptability and acceptance as well.

It is important that a child grows in confidence day by day and that as parents we do all we can to encourage confidence and self-worth in all situations.

The early years foundation stage is a statutory assessment and therefore all five year olds will go through this, but it should be done in such a way that the child is unaware. The emphasis and reason for bringing this to your attention is to prepare parents for what is being looked for by the education system. You may agree with me that it feels like the education system is setting up children with autism to fail, by making so many of the standards difficult to achieve. Looking at it from a different perspective, I think it can be a helpful tool to have conversations with your child's teacher.

Remember you know your child best. Take this as an opportunity to guide the teachers in the best way they can support your child. The ultimate aim should be that if at all possible children are educated together, and therefore this will require some teachers and education institutions to be more flexible in their approach.

Summary on early years standards and autism

- Advise the assessor on the best way to give instructions to your child.

- Take the time to explain the body language your child uses and what this means.

- It is important that you explain the specific needs of your child.

- Ask about the setting's inclusivity policy.

Conversations with professionals

The early years foundation stage was not in place when James started school. If it had been I would have had the following conversation with James' teacher:

"Firstly, James does listen to everything that goes on. You might not know this as he will not look at you, but the lack of eye contact is a way of being able to listen. James' hearing is exceptional but in a classroom this means that he will get easily distracted with other noises, and therefore I would advise that James sit near the front to give him the best chance of hearing what you have to say.

Secondly, James is able to follow instructions but these need to be clear and simple. If you ask for him to do too many steps in one go then he will shut down on the task.

James will talk to you about what he has been doing, for example over the weekend, but this will be in very matter of fact terms. He is unlikely to talk about future events as he needs a lot of time to prepare for these, and if you ask what he might do over the summer holidays this could cause quite a degree of anxiety if he is unable to say or explain.

James is fabulous at ball games and has great hand to eye coordination.

I know it is unlikely that James is going to have to dress himself, but you need to be aware that he struggles with his shoes and may take a long time to get them right. Please be patient with him.

James is very independent and is happy to do activities that he is familiar with. Please note that if you are introducing something new then it would be great if I could know in advance and then I can take some time at home to explain this to him.

James will not tell you if he is struggling to understand something; he will just stop doing it. James will just walk away from a task and will not know that this is inappropriate. Please do not think that he is doing this because of rudeness. He is likely to be doing this because he is struggling with the task.

James can become quite fixated and absorbed on certain games. For example, if you are asking the children to build a train track going through a town, then he will become absorbed with the trains and their wheels or with the cars. I would advise that you are very specific about what you want James to do and for how long.

James is great at reading and enjoys certain books. He will write, but this is not his favourite thing to do. Also he can count well.

The last thing I think you need to be aware of is that James struggles with imaginative play. He plays all the time but does not get the concept of role play or acting another character. For example, we have tried being different animals on a farmyard, but James will not engage with this at all. He knows the noises that each animal makes but does not understand why we would want to mimic them!

Please can we come to some agreement about free dress or dress up days as this will cause a significant amount of anxiety for James."

If I had had this conversation and subsequent conversations year on year, we would have avoided many of the difficulties we encountered with the education system, such as unnecessary assessments for hearing loss, traumas over dressing up days at school, anxiety over school trips, stressful summer holidays preparing for the following school year and so on.

Each child with autism will have different ways of expressing themselves and different things that they are able to do confidently. I think we can expect that teachers have a general awareness of autism; the danger is that there can be an assumption by some professionals that all children with autism will have the same challenges. You are the expert on your child, so own this expertise and take the time to explain to the teacher how you can best work together to support your son or daughter.

If you start this in year one, then as your child gets older you will be more confident in talking to the different teachers. Also when you hit a difficult issue like homework then you have a better chance of coming to a successful resolution.

Remember each year 190 days of your child's life is at school. That is 52% of their time, more than half of every year for thirteen or fourteen years. In the best interests of your son or daughter it is so important that you see school as your partner. However, as a partnership it does not start off on an equal footing. The school know nothing about the unique nature of your child. Seek to work together on providing the best possible support for your child.

Section Four
Small things make a big difference

"I have seen and met angels disguised as ordinary people living ordinary lives"

Tracy Chapman

Socialising and school

In school, James' strategy was to remain quiet and sit next to people who will tell him what he needs to do. To an extent this worked well. However at parents' evenings the teachers advised James to raise his hand to ask when he didn't understand and needed instruction on a topic that has been covered. James never did do this. He just came home and told me he didn't understand something and we used to go through it together.

This approach got more difficult as James moved through the years, since the teaching methods, particularly in maths, had changed so much from my school days. The frustration mounted as I was in danger of confusing him further. James was adamant that he did not want to tell his teachers his difficulties and he certainly didn't want me to talk to them.

I think it is due to James' resilience that he coped so well with school. He developed strategies to manage the things that stressed him. Physical Education (PE) was the most challenging for him due to the potential contact. I can't comment on the social side of school as James would never say and school never said that he spent a lot of his time on his own. But I do know that James was always the first child out when the school bell sounded, he was always on his own and he would never invite another school friend round to the house, even though I tried to persuade him on many occasions. I later found out that this was because 'friends are for school and home is home'.

I tried to get James to join Saturday clubs, such as football and bowling, but he refused. There was a short stint during this period when he did agree to a Saturday tennis club and a badminton club. Unfortunately the badminton club ran out of funding and stopped. The tennis didn't work out because the trainers couldn't understand why James would stand and wait for the ball to come to him rather than run for it! This was an interesting manifestation of the autistic trait of being literal! The instruction had been 'You hit the ball back when it comes to you!' if they had said 'Chase the ball to hit it when it comes over the net', we might have had more success!

Socially

Ages 6-10 for most children are about learning the social norms, forming, breaking and reforming friendships. For a child on the autism spectrum this is very different. As a general rule, children with autism are very matter of fact and sometimes struggle with the slight nuances of friendships.

Certainly a child with autism will remain distant from social bonding and quite often will prefer the company of adults to other children their own age.

Typically children of this age are developing their creative minds and imaginative play. This is a common difficulty for children with autism as they see the world in set, concrete and fixed terms and do not accept that there might be value in imagining something else.

This way of playing which can be quite solitary and repetitive can isolate a child even further from other children whose natural development is seeking to explore alternatives through imagination.

I am acutely aware of the importance of social interaction and friendships but these cannot be forced. I had to keep reminding myself that this situation upset others, but it did not upset James. If James was happy then why worry about something that is not going to change? If it was forced to change it would result in unhappiness.

The lesson repeats itself:

Effective parenting is about enabling the child to be happy, not the adult.

I know lots of people that hold onto their expectations about what is right and wrong and what a child should and should not experience.

This is where the difference is: raising a child with autism requires a parent to suspend all their expectations and focus on the individual child and what makes them happy.

There is of course the long term view to consider, that a parent's responsibility is to prepare a child for adult life. There is of course some balance to be sought, and every child, indeed everybody, has to do some things that they don't like. The key to this is finding where the compromise is.

Summary of school and socialising

- Be prepared to put in a lot of time in reinforcing school activities and supporting with homework.

- Make sure you understand the school teaching methods. Teachers are usually quite happy to go through this with parents.

- Typical development phases for children of 6-11 are around social interaction and creative and imaginative play.

- Remember the use of specific language will help your child understand what is required in certain activities.

- A parent's job is to enable their child to be happy.

- It is not necessary to force social situations.

Holidays

I persevered with holidays for around ten years. I was hopeful that the more I subjected James to holidays the easier it would become.

'The first sign of insanity is to keep doing the same thing and hoping for a different result!'

My perseverance was just false hope, as the reality was that there would be 358 full days between each holiday.

That is 358 days of a set comfortable routine for James.

358 days of James knowing what to expect.

358 days of being in an environment that is safe and secure.

For me to think that James would get used to a seven day blip on the landscape was deluded. The destination is unknown, requires a significant journey, the weather is different, the people are different, the food is different, the activities during the day are different. How could this cause anything other than stress?

The light dawned on me in 2004 and that was the last holiday we had.

Other children who experience autism might be perfectly ok with holidays. It is just that it didn't work for James. I think if there had been one place that we went to on holiday then the experience might have been different, but hindsight is a wonderful thing.

One of the major problems we had was that James would want exact details about what the place would be like, how long the journey would take, how many people would be there.

As I couldn't provide concrete answers for these questions then the anxiety levels rose. For James as anxiety rises then the other senses go into overdrive as well.

The pattern building up to holidays was lots of questions, frustration with the lack of concrete answers, more questions, more frustration, leading to more anxiety, leading to more questions, leading to anger at the responses, leading to behaviours / obsessions around food, cleanliness and clothing, leading to more anxiety, leading to explosions of anger.

This was just the build up to the holiday. The journeys were a little calmer and the actual holidays themselves were interspersed with the behaviour patterns above.

Would you subject your child to this just for the sake of a holiday? It certainly wasn't a 'holiday'.

So the reality is that we now have 'relax days' where James does whatever James wants to do with his time. This would invariably mean playing Spyro or Mario on the gamecube/Wii, as it is now known.

I would attempt to divert James with other games with his cars and tractors. We have always had dogs, so some doggie time on the park was always good. The aim as a parent was to enable my son to be as happy and relaxed as possible.

Christmas and birthdays

It was not until age three or four when James realised that there were two days in the year where things were dramatically different; his birthday and Christmas day. It was not until he was aged seven or eight that I realised the change in behaviour in April and December was directly linked to these two days! Invariably this was about a ten day build-up of anxiety.

It first manifests as irritability and then bursts of anger, then aggression at seemingly random things. James was unable to articulate what was frustrating him. By observing the patterns over a number of years it became clear that the event was the issue.

The day itself was also problematic, in a variety of ways, ranging from constant questions about what would happen when, to refusal to do things, to throwing presents around because they do not do what James expects them to do, to not wanting to wait for items to be built, assembled or constructed. I even resorted to unwrapping, assembling and rewrapping presents before Christmas or birthdays so they were ready instantly.

Over the years I emotionally and practically prepared myself for these events so that they could be as stress free as possible. The difficulty arose when friends or work colleagues would ask how things had gone. I would just say 'Yes it was a lovely day thanks'. The reality was very different. But the days after the 'event' were always pleasant and much calmer and those were the times I looked forward to.

Affection

The hardest thing for me to deal with is not being able to give James a hug, a cuddle or a kiss. Some children with autism are not touch sensitive and therefore this is not an issue. James is, however, and all I can do is verbally reassure him, but this has to be at a distance.

Just to touch James' shoulder results in a shudder through him. I can get an angry or violent response if I touch his hair, and I would never be able to remove a loose eye lash. I tell James that I love him, but I have only ever heard this back from him on one occasion.

It brought me to tears.

It is emotionally very difficult raising a child with autism, but it brings its special gifts as well. The small things like an unexpected smile brings joy to my heart. The straightforward blunt observations make me laugh so much. I am so very proud of his achievements because they are worked for so hard.

Moving

You might think that moving would be a cause for great anxiety. However the way I managed this was by ensuring that James' room was identical in each house that we lived in. We have moved eight times and the pattern that worked for us was talking about what the new house is like, seeing the new house before we move, James choosing which room will be his, talking each day about what it will be like, what will be the same and what will be different.

On move day James has either been at school or at his Grandma's. James' room is the first to be sorted with all boxes unpacked, bed ready and items exactly where they were in the previous house. I do mean 'exactly' i.e. X marks the spot on the table where certain items are placed. James then comes home and checks that everything is as I said it would be. I have to allow at least an hour of uninterrupted time to be with James to help make any tweaks in his room that are necessary and then James is settled. I then get on with the rest of the house.

The other aspect that has never changed in all the moves we have made is that James' school has remained the same. When we moved in with my partner we moved out of the county and we were 40 miles away from school. I got permission from the school for James to remain there. Remember, the school do not know that James is on the autism spectrum, I just had to explain in relation to James' settling and continuing to make good progress. So from a five minute walk to school James had a 45 minute drive to school. It was a new routine but James coped well. I am constantly amazed at the things that James copes with. Some of the things that I think will cause greatest anxiety result in no reaction at all. Other things that I do not even consider to be an issue are huge for him.

Summary of holidays, affection and moving

- If changes in routine affect the anxiety levels of your child, then keep things such as holidays the same.

- Rather than holidays, 'relax days' can be just as effective.

- Don't worry about what other people think.

- Remember a 'holiday' is about being as happy and relaxed as possible.

- When it comes to affection remind yourself whether the need is yours or your child's.

- Parenting a child with autism spectrum can be emotionally very difficult. Find someone to be your rock.

- Find beauty and joy in the small things; there are many of them.

- Expect the unexpected - things will change just when you think you know what to do!

- Success is all about taking time, being prepared, listening, talking, understanding and finding empathy.

Personal reflections on the period 6 - 11 years

It is usual for children during these years to be experimenting with relationships and friendships. This is not the case for some children with autism. I learnt that this is ok.

You cannot force things to be something they are not just because it is the norm. There is a lot of beauty in doing things a different way. It is good to be different.

Seeking happiness in the things that make us happy is more important.

I think there is so much that society in general can learn from people who experience autism. One of the biggest lessons will be the ability to focus on what is important to you.

Holidays are an invented construct and they are not something that all people enjoy or want to do. This does not make people odd, it means that some people know what makes them happy. These people will follow that path regardless of the norm that has been created.

I learnt that some of the big things that I would think would be stressful, have no negative impact whatsoever on James. There is a joy in being kept on your toes!

I learnt as a parent to maintain a belief in what you know to be right and to remain strong in the face of resistance.

I continue to fully appreciate all the love and stability that my mother provides. She understands and believes that anything is possible. She is always there for us and always puts her grandson first. Whoever it is, find someone to be a rock for you.

Section Five
Getting older

"You see things and say 'why?'
But I dream things that never were and say
'why not?' "

George Bernard Shaw

Teenagers

Normal teenage development can feel anything but normal to parents.

When thinking about children and how they develop emotionally, socially and physically over the years it is astounding the full range of development that occurs in the early years from 0-5. Ages 6-10 are more of a consolidation phase where most children are developing on a social and emotional level. But fast forward to the teenage years and it all goes haywire again.

There is the emotional turmoil that teenagers go through particularly with the chemical and hormonal changes that are occurring for them.

Then there are the social developments, the influence of peers, the media, as well as family that they are subjected to. There is the search for their 'identity' and the pushing of boundaries in the process.

For some there is the infallibility stage where they take risks without any concern for the consequences.

This is all normal.

Is this the case for teenagers with autism? Absolutely yes.

Their bodies go through all the natural changes that any other child goes through. The primary divergence from normal teenage development I have noticed is in social development. In this area I have witnessed that friends, family and the media have had little or no effect on the desire or willingness to socialise.

By age thirteen I had a fairly good idea of the triggers for anxiety and stress, but from fourteen to sixteen years I was unclear whether the triggers related to autism or hormones.

When I was confused my only option was to put it down to hormonal changes.

James' reactions appeared to be intensified. I think I perceived this because of the physical changes evident in him, changing from a boy to a 6'2" young man in one year.

One year I was able to contain the aggressive outbursts, and the next I had a towering teenager who was angry and who had the power to throw things and damage the walls. It was overwhelming.

I was fortunate that the outbursts were less frequent as James grew older, but they were still there. My strategy was to ensure that his room was as safe as possible, with limited number of items that were free standing and able to be used as throwing objects.

It was the physical changes that brought the most challenges. The emotional changes were the same as any teenager. The divergence from other teenagers was in the area of social development, of pushing boundaries and trying out new experiences.

James and other young adults with autism can be very matter of fact. When we have talked about drugs, alcohol and cigarettes and their dangers, James' response was: 'I don't know why you are talking to me about this, they are disgusting and I wouldn't go anywhere near them'.

When I asked what they had covered in sex education at school, the response was very matter of fact and I know that with James' touch sensitivity he hasn't to date wanted to be touched by anyone else, let alone have a girlfriend.

So for quite a lot of parents of teenagers who worry about their son or daughter staying out late at night and what they may or may not be doing, this just hasn't been a factor for me. James is quite happy doing the things that James does.

Routines

The routine during the teenage years was fairly static, with getting up at 7.30am, walking to school for 8.30am, walking home at 4pm, followed by dinner, homework, relax time and bed by 9pm.

Weekend routines were get up around 10am (later and later as the years passed). Play tennis or badminton. Walk the dogs and in the evenings, playing on the computer and watching TV.

For six years this didn't change, and in it not changing and James being settled and comfortable with this routine, then the periods of anger and aggression became less and less.

James was reluctant to change this routine and indeed would get angry at the suggestion of change. One small example of this is when it rained. I would offer to drive James to school. This used to cause much anxiety and resultant anger and consequently his school day did not start well.

Living such a fixed routine can present specific challenges for parents, particularly if there are other children in the family. What I have described would be inordinately difficult, unless there was a very supportive family member or friend that can help maintain the established routine and still allow the other children opportunities to have variety in their lives. I know what I am describing is not that easy for some.

Other people's judgements about personal lifestyle choices was something I hadn't anticipated. Firstly, because I never labelled James, I could never say at the end of a summer break, 'No we didn't go anywhere this summer because James has autism'. I used to say, 'We like to stay at home during the holidays'.

You can see that some people just don't understand this and they have a particular view of you and your family because of it. Having a label can help other people understand. However you then have to question whether you are getting a diagnosis for the best support for your child or to allay other people's prejudice.

School trips were another blip on the horizon of relative calm dominated by established routines. James understood that these were required, and he did go on the school trips. The day itself would go well, but the preceding days were dominated by frustration for James. I would not be able to answer any of his questions about:

- SPECIFICALLY where they were going

- what time they would set off

- Who would be on the coach

- how long the journey would take

- what they would do during the day and so on

With school comes the requirement for homework. I would attempt to help James with all his subjects (geology being the most difficult!). The levels of anxiety would escalate the more I did not know the answers. We would endeavour to research the topic on the internet but the skill in searching the web is knowing what you are looking for; as James had not understood the instructions from school this made it exceptionally difficult to search for the correct things.

I remember that I used to sigh with relief when James said there was no homework. That meant no stress, anxiety or anger that evening. We went through this routine for the whole of James' secondary (high) school years.

We did a lot of preparation for the GCSE exams and James was very successful. I am so proud of him, because it took a lot for him to remain calm in the exam situation and concentrate of what the question might be asking him. Other than the discussions around timings for the exam and where James would sit, the main focus of the preparation was on the best way to answer the questions. It would be very easy for someone with autism to just give a very direct, short answer. So we worked hard on how to write everything related to that topic even though the question might not appear to ask that. This is a difficult concept for people who interpret things literally.

I have to include a quote from Albert Einstein here as it is something I vehemently believe.

"Everyone is a genius. But if you judge a fish by its ability to climb a tree it will spend a lifetime thinking it is stupid."
Albert Einstein.

The parenting technique I deployed here was surrounding the fish in a bubble of water, pulling them up the tree and after that achievement the fish can shine in its real genius.

These teenage years were ones of relative calm. The episodes of frustration, anger and aggression became less. But when they did happen they were challenging because of James' physical strength and height. I ask myself why would this period be calmer? Is it because James is learning more coping strategies? Is it that generally James is feeling less challenged by his environment? Or is it that there are some biological changes that are contributing to the calmness?

There is a wealth of research on the subject of autism, and it is not my intention to comment on these but to give my view through experiencing this with my son. From this perspective

I believe that the more a parent can suspend their view of societal norms and release themselves from these expectations, the easier the journey will be. If you can allow a child to have an established routine that they feel comfortable with, they are likely to be less stressed. The fewer demands we can place on a child to do things that we want to do, then the more stable, safe and secure they will become.

What I have learnt during the teenage years?

• Maintaining a routine that works for your child, regardless of other people and society's expectations, really does work.

• Don't let a physical change make a problem seem worse than it is. Actually things are getting better.

• Do all you can as a parent to enable the genius in your child to shine.

That star is really starting to shine within James and he is flourishing in the young adult he is becoming.

School is out!

School is finished; the years of established routines coming to an end. The transition between school and post 16 options would always be eventful. I hadn't quite anticipated what would happen, but then one should always expect the unexpected.

James was quite clear that he would like to stay on at school which meant doing 'A' levels. I think James was under the impression that 6th Form would be the same as secondary school.

Certainly the physical environment was the same and most of the students stayed on. As for the routine, well, that was a surprise to both James and me.

September arrived and the start of the 6th form began. There was the usual build-up of anxiety about where to register and who would be in his form group, what they would be covering in the subjects and how the week would be structured.

The first day came along and was very similar to the previous years, but by the end of week one it was becoming increasingly obvious that 6th form would be a completely different experience.

The college approach was that students in years 12 and 13 should be able to direct their own learning. Three quarters of the timetable was self-directed study in the library or from home or any other quiet place of choice.

The lessons were very different with teachers often not attending and students expected to work under their own direction. Also there were of course the 'free periods'. For someone with autism this lack of structure on all levels was extremely bewildering.

This bewilderment led to frustration, which led to anger.

Together James and I worked on what he should do in the self-directed learning slots and in the free periods. Luckily we lived close enough to the school for James to have his free periods at home.

In one of the free slots, James spent time with a friend and they were on the computer looking at different sites which were making them laugh. A teacher entered the room and asked James and his friend to stop what they were doing and concentrate on some work. James just responded, 'This is a free period I can do what I like'.

As you can imagine this didn't go down well with the teacher. I had a letter from the school explaining the situation and saying what the punishment was going to be, namely that James could not go into the computer room until the next new term in six weeks.

This episode highlighted a number of difficulties. In the first instance it was apparent that the lack of structure was impeding James' ability to settle. Secondly, the school's completely unhelpful response to my intervention was a direct consequence of me never telling them that James has autism. I had tried to explain to the head of year that James' response to the teacher was just a matter of fact response, which in actuality was factually correct.

The school would not budge on their decision that it was just rudeness and maintained the punishment.

The punishment caused two things; firstly that James now did not know where to go or what to do with his free time and it caused James great anger as he could not understand why he was treated like this.

I therefore had six weeks of anger and frustration to deal with. I wrote to the teacher concerned outlining the nature of James' needs and requesting the position to be reconsidered. They would not move.

I suggested that they were being discriminatory against James, which they ignored. If I had been more determined I would have taken the matter further, but all my energy was being taken by dealing with the anxiety over the ensuing weeks.

The irony in the whole situation was that I was actually really pleased that James was socialising with someone at school and that they were having a good time. The 6th form managed to remove all that pleasure from both of us! All because they couldn't tolerate a teacher being spoken to by a student in a manner considered to be rude.

The next term was devoted to preparing for the 'AS' level exams. This was a similar situation to the preparation for the GCSE exams but the content was more detailed, which in itself was not the problem. The issue was the style of answering required to the questions presented in the exam papers. If the questions had been fact based rather than compare, contrast and present an opinion James would have faired better. We did hours of revision and preparation, and James felt after the exams that he had answered the questions in detail and was quite happy with his work. However when the results came in he had not passed any of his written exams. This was a devastating blow as James was confident in what he had done.

We had another few weeks of frustration due to a lack of understanding of the results.

Once James was calm enough for a conversation we discussed some of the options. I was clear that I felt that James should not resit or retake the year. I outlined what we had experienced over the year and asked James whether he really wanted to continue for another two years with it. Thankfully, after time, he agreed. The remaining options were full time paid work or an apprenticeship.

James was keen to get a qualification so opted for the apprenticeship route. Over the next two weeks, without me knowing, James investigated which qualification he would like to get and chose creative and digital media.

James had made this decision in enough time for us to be able to attend a local college open day.

(A reminder of your frame of reference for reading this: a young man with autism where change of routine is an issue and change of environment is an issue combined with a 17 year old who has just found out that he has failed something for the first time, is feeling dejected, unmotivated and unconfident.)

We attend the local college, which is only seven miles away, but is located in one of the most deprived areas in the county. The college has clearly been under funded for many years with the building in need of significant repair. The journey would require two buses to get there. On entering the college little thought or preparation had gone into how to direct people to the correct place. When we did eventually find someone to ask about where we should go, we were left to find our own way down a number of dark corridors, where we felt like we were going into some dungeon type environment. James was silent when we found the room and was clearly uncomfortable with it.

After waiting 25 minutes outside the classroom the tutor invited us in and asked why James wanted to do the course, what he would bring, saying that he expected all students to give a weekly presentation on work that they were doing and finishing his speech off with ,My course is always over-subscribed, if you decide to apply you need to know that I turn away 70% of applicants'. We left. What can you say to that?

I made a written complaint to the head of the college about the full range of things that we experienced, the most appalling being the way an under-confident teenager was spoken to when they were showing initiative about attending college. I had no response. I told James that regardless of how he felt, I was not allowing him to attend that college. James was just relieved that he didn't have to go again.

We then looked at other colleges in a commutable distance and encountered many problems, from the college not offering the course, the course no longer running, or the journey being unmanageable at over three hours. We then changed track and looked at providers of apprenticeships who came out to the workplace rather than having to attend college. BINGO! We found a reasonably local college that did just that and once a job had been found then they would assess the work of the student in the workplace.

Our next challenge was to find an employer offering a job that was to do with creative and digital media. There were none on the apprenticeship website, none in the papers, and none at the local youth centre.

Time was running out and James needed to get a routine established as soon as possible.

The answer was staring me in the face. James could work for me. Not ideal in terms of the social aspect of working, but certainly good in terms of getting started with the concept of working and starting the college element. I checked that it was ok with the college that he work in a family business and this was fine. So James started straight away.

Ordinarily this would be a perfect solution, however the nature of autism is that some children compartmentalise things. The challenge that we faced was that James could not see me as an employer; I am his mum and will always be his mum.

I continued to work hard on making the distinction that while in this room, on this computer, we are at work and this requires different behaviour. On the plus side James produced marvellous work. He managed the website, all the links and the social media.

His assessor was very pleased with the work that he was producing. James was observed in the office undertaking tasks that had been given that day. The major advantage was that I knew the language to use to explain things and I ensured that James had understood before I left him to a task. If only all employers could do this, there would be so many more opportunities for people.

James' assessor became aware that he had a YouTube channel that combined his love of music with his knowledge of computers.

The assessor could see that James had 58,000 subscribers at the time. On average his tracks were downloaded 200,000 times each. He had monetised these tracks and was gaining an income from his passion. The assessor encouraged James to use his channel for the qualification. Over the two years it took to do the apprenticeship his channel grew to over 250,000 subscribers and millions of views on his videos.

In 2014 James was awarded IT Apprentice of the year.

Where did it start and what for the future?

Our journey began when James was born at 6.15am one Thursday morning in April 1995. It was to be the hottest summer for many years, the sun was shining that morning and it didn't stop for months. It was beautiful.

Sitting here 21 years later, reflecting on what has gone, I realise what an amazing journey we are having. There is a long way to go but I have learnt so much through the tears, traumas, triumphs and tender moments that my son and I have shared.

James is flourishing.

He hopes to live in a small flat or house on his own. He is torn between urban and rural living. We have done both and James loves the peace and quiet of the countryside, but dislikes the poor internet connection! And the spiders! He likes towns because of the new houses, the good internet services but dislikes the people. A decision he will make in his own time.

It is still one day at a time and we enjoy each day for what it brings.

Final thought from James' Grandma

Early on as he looked around
Upwards was a whispering sound
Swaying, shimmering gold and green
A better sight could not be seen.
The trees were nature at its best and
Always helped in getting rest.

E.A.Lees (Grandma extraordinaire)

Jargon you may come across

ABA Applied Behaviour Analysis.

ADD (Attention Deficit Disorder) Poor attention without over activity.

ADOS Autism Diagnostic Observation Schedule.

ADHD (Attention Deficit Hyperactivity Disorder) Poor attention with marked over activity, as opposed to Hyperkinetic Disorder which is overactivity without poor attention

Asperger's Syndrome Autism without the speech delay.

Atypical autism Behaviour pattern that fits most but not all of the criteria for typical autism.

Conduct disorder or oppositional difficulty disorder Challenging behaviour that cannot be explained.

DAMP Disorder of Attention, Motor coordination and Perception, e.g. dyslexia and dyspraxia together.

Dyslexia Perception and reading difficulties.

Dyspraxia Difficulties coordinating movements (this is sometimes called developmental coordination disorder or motor coordination disorder).

GCD Gluten and Casein free Diet.

High functioning autism Behaviour that fits some of the autism criteria with only some negative effect on daily living.

Hyperkinetic disorder See ADHD above

Neuro-diverse .v. Neuro-typical Autistic .v. average person. Neuro-diverse is a less stereotypical and stigmatised word that is actually more accurate in its description of the condition.

Proprioception The ability to sense stimuli arising within the body regarding position, motion, and equilibrium.

Savant A person demonstrating exceptional skills or brilliance in specific areas, such as rapid calculation, art, memory, or musical ability.

Semantic–pragmatic disorder Socially inappropriate use of language.

Tourette's syndrome Sudden involuntary jerky movements and vocal noises that cannot be controlled.

If you are at all concerned about your child and would like some professional advice, please see your doctor in the first instance.

You will need to describe in detail what you are worried about. They will use their judgement about whether what you describe is within normal ranges or whether there will be a referral for further assessment from a paediatrician or specialist team.

About the author: Bebe Boyse

Bebe Boyse was born and raised in North Yorkshire, England. She is a single mum to James and throughout her working career has specialised in working with children, young people and families. After completing her Honours degree in Psychology at Plymouth University, Bebe spent two years in New York working with people with mental health problems.

On returning to London in the early 1990s, Bebe set up, ran and was managing director of a supported employment service for people with learning difficulties and disabilities. This was one of the first three in the UK. She then moved on to enable the closure of hospital provision for people with learning disabilities and in doing so specialised in developing the workforce to be equipped to provide inclusive support to people in the community. This time was interspersed with being practice lecturer at Thames Valley University. The late 1990s and into the 2000s was focused on developing the workforce who supported young people and families.

Since 2013 Bebe has focused on the desire to share her knowledge and experience from her professional career and her parenting experiences with others.

You can follow Bebe Boyse on:

Facebook: Spectrum parenting
Resources available: www.spectrumparenting.net
Email: info@spectrumparenting.net

Other books from Spring Publishing

Steering the Mothership: The Complexities of Mothering
Lisa Cherry   ISBN 978-0992758714

What if you didn't get the mother you wanted? What if you couldn't be the mother you wanted to be? The stories in this book illustrate the real-life complexities of motherhood. They help every reader to understand their own journey, both as a child and as a mother and help them investigate the single relationship that affects us most throughout our lives, whether it has been a positive or a negative experience.

It is essential reading for anyone working in Early Years Development, Social Work or Education, or simply trying to understand this profound relationship.

Face to Face in the Workplace: A Handbook of Strategies for Effective Discussions
Julie Cooper   ISBN 978-0955968037

Looking to improve your people management skills? This is an accessible guide to every meeting, discussion or difficult conversation you will need to have.

Written for busy people who need quick solutions, Face to Face in the Workplace will equip you with all the tools and strategies you'll need to get it right every time.

You will: have more productive discussions that please everyone involved; save time by knowing how to prepare effectively; never have to worry about what to say in difficult meetings; learn to get your point over more effectively.

The One to One Toolkit: Tips and Strategies for Advisers, Coaches and Mentors

Julie Cooper and Ann Reynolds   ISBN 978-0955968051

Does your job involve helping people to move forward in their career, learning, or personal development? If so, this book is for you. It aims to meet the needs of people employed in the field of advice and guidance in a practical, user friendly way.

It explains useful models, suggests strategies for dealing with difficulties, and provides powerful, memorable tools to use with clients.

The Groupwork Toolkit: How To Convert Your One To One Advice Skills To Work With Groups

Ann Reynolds and Julie Cooper   ISBN 978-0955968013

The Groupwork Toolkit makes groupwork easy for anyone used to working one to one, by showing you how to recognise and transfer the skills you already have.

Advisers, coaches and mentors have a wealth of interpersonal and communication skills, but may lack the experience and confidence to transfer them successfully to running groups. The Groupwork Toolkit can help.

It demystifies group work, and gives you the confidence and knowledge you need to facilitate groups, whether your group are learning new skills, or have come for advice or guidance. It explains how you can deliver brilliant groupwork by planning well, setting objectives and using a variety of training techniques.

The Job Interview Toolkit: Exercises to get you fit for your interview

by Ann Reynolds and Julie Cooper   ISBN 978-0955968020

The Job Interview Toolkit is a practical, easy to follow guide to preparing for interviews, ideal for job seekers of all ages, especially the young and those returning to work after a break.

It contains a selection of activities, organised in the five-step TAPAS programme, designed to get you fit to perform like a star on the day. Its easy to read format make it accessible to job seekers of all ages. Advisers will find ideas for working with their clients too.

This book is:

Easy to read – short sections, illustrations and diagrams, examples and danger stories.

Practical – with things to do, questions to answer, photos to comment on, things to practise with a friend. Most of us learn best by doing, so you will find a five-step programme of exercises to get you fit and ready for the interview (the really important facts are there too).

A simple framework that is easy to learn:T-A-P-A-S.

Think   –   Analyse   –   Prepare   –   Adjust   –   Shine!

This book will make sure you know what to do, perform at your best and sell yourself brilliantly!